To Bryn, Jo and all
Richmond staff,
Once you've read n
know I'm mad!

If I could give you all one
(a copy of the book), I would.

I love you all: Kim, Anna, Sarah,
Emma, Swan, Zoe ...
   Sorry for any omissions ....
(add names here) ...

Even Phil, Joe and Jack ...
   and if I've missed anyone, it's
because I'm pissed ...

I love you all without exception.
Because love is free and
   hatred is costly.
      David.   17·10·10.

THE LIGHT, THE DARKNESS, AND THE COLOURS

A Spiritual Journey

David Wilding

authorHOUSE®

AuthorHouse™ UK Ltd.
500 Avebury Boulevard
Central Milton Keynes, MK9 2BE
www.authorhouse.co.uk
Phone: 08001974150

©2010 David Wilding. All rights reserved.

No part of this book may be reproduced, stored in a retrieval system, or transmitted by any means without the written permission of the author.

First published by AuthorHouse   9/29/2010

ISBN: 978-1-4520-0838-7 (sc)

This book is printed on acid-free paper.

CONTENTS

Introduction 1
Where Is God? 3
Politics, Economics, Greed,
The Environment And Mental Illness 4
Money 6
Masters Of The Universe 7
The Greedy Man 8
Cod War 9
The Tramp 10
Declaration Of Intent And Faith 12
The Prophet 14
May You 17
Prophecy 18
The Mystery 19
Who Are You To Judge? 20
A Religious Gathering 22
The Moral Maze 24
Good, Evil And Satan 27
Mr. Hitler 30
Satan 31
Things Satanic 33
The 20th Century. Satan's Victory & The Birth Of The New Age 34
Just Desserts 38
Time Gentlemen (And Ladies) PlEase 39
The Daily Nonsense 41
End Of Time (Ism) 43
Re-Ignition 46
I Might Have Been 47
Passing By 48

Days 49
"Prepare For The Second Coming" 50
The Angel Of Death.. 51
And Now For Something Completely Different! The Colours 52
A New Year Message (2008) From: 53
We're All Bonkers Now 54
Food, Glorious Food! 55
Living In Devon 57
Gorbachev 58
Fight Night.. 61
The Jesus Joke Book! 62
Fat Cat 63
Rupert And The Au Pair 64
The Fridge Monster 65
Camilla (The Gorilla) 66
The Bleeding Doctor.. 67
Proverbs 68
Jerusalem 69

INTRODUCTION

Religion is a powerful psychological instrument. The belief in a God, active in the world, delivering favours selectively, has a profound impact upon the behaviour of religious adherents. Get on the right side of God and things should go well. Get on the wrong side and things might turn out badly.

Then there's death. God has the ability to recreate you after death if you adhere to the correct code of conduct, belief or if you deserve it.

Because of these powerful psychological factors religion can assume the status of, well, a religion. Something really important to be defended with tenacity and that's when problems arise. Problems such as prejudice, superiority, maybe feelings of immortality, belligerence and arrogance.

Yet religious values can also generate good attitudes such as compassion, commitment, charity, a sense of purpose and worth, responsibility, empathy and good conduct. So it's not all negative!

I am intrigued by the role religion and belief-systems have played in the world ever since people discerned a need for such beliefs. Ideas of good and evil, divine intervention, the outcome of events determined by supernatural forces and so on. History says that religion is important and it remains important in the minds of many people today.

It's easy to take religion a tad too seriously, and I have done, but thank goodness that I can laugh at some of the absurdities too.

So this book is a product of my 'spiritual journey and enlightenment.' Sometimes it reflects the darkness of my thoughts but thank God, if He exists, for the lighter and brighter thoughts too.

O.K. so let me enlighten you. I do believe that there is a God, almost certainly, probably, but then again maybe I'm wrong.

I do believe that people can be on the receiving end of 'divine inspiration' but I also accept that certain mental processes can lead to delusions. Miracles may happen too.

I also believe that Jesus Christ was a 'man of God'. He claimed also to be the 'Son of God'. My faith says that is true but I can't conclusively prove it.

So what you will find in this book is a mixture of certainty and an element of doubt. If your faith is different or stronger than mine, hopefully you will 'forgive' what you may perceive as 'errors'. If you don't forgive me, then kindly get lost.

As for the all too frequent notion amongst religious believers that the world will end one day, time will cease and there will be a spectacular judgement, renewal and perfection of all creation. It's possible, I suppose, but should we worry? But we do need to worry about the 'state of the world' because by our own beliefs and actions we can determine possible outcomes.

So I shall open my ramblings and writings with 'Where Is God?' a very definite 'God does exist' moment.

Then I shall take you on the roller-coaster of my 'spiritual journey'. I hope it doesn't bore, perplex or anger you. If it does have a glass of something strong or a cup of tea and a biscuit.

WHERE IS GOD?

Where is God when you need him?
Why doesn't he answer our prayers.
Where is God when you need him,
Isn't he concerned with human affairs?
I'll tell you where God is!
He's there in your suffering and there in your pain,
he's there yesterday, tomorrow and there once again.
He's there in your mourning and there in your grief
He's there in the morning and there in your belief.
He's not there when you get petulant and make demands
He's not there in your arrogance and at your commands.
He's there when you're desperate and when you're alone,
He's there to comfort you, though not at the end of a moan.
He's there in your achievements and there in your success
He's there when you seek justice and adequate redress.
He's incredible and loving and mighty and kind.
To have missed him, not seen him, perhaps you are blind.
Blind to his love and blind to his care,
So say, "Thanks and please," I ask you to dare.

David   θ

Because God is amazing.

POLITICS, ECONOMICS, GREED, THE ENVIRONMENT AND MENTAL ILLNESS

Ever since I studied economics at college I have been interested in the political scene. 'Boring', some of you might think and sometimes it can be. Subsequently I graduated in economics from Sheffield University.

The recent financial crisis has been intriguing even for those who find such matters really rather boring. Just how much power do the people with vast amounts of money have? Should we leave them free to exploit that power? Is there anything we can do to 'rein them in?'

The short and simple answer is: Yes they could be reined in but only through international cooperation and co-ordination of financial policies, which some people would disagree with often because of vested interests.

The poems: 'Money', 'Masters of the Universe' and 'The Greedy Man' are self-explanatory.

One of the matters which has become of international concern in recent years is the environmental issue. 'Greed economics' seems to set no boundaries on the exploitation of the planet. Some people foresee an environmental catastrophe. Although scientists cannot conclusively prove that any apparent global warming is man-made it does seem logical to believe that there is a limit to how far human exploitation of the planet can continue. With the human population set to rise above 7 billion and the demands for economic prosperity rising across the globe, what are the environmental implications? I do not have a crystal ball to see into the future but it is worrying.

We have overfished the oceans, polluted the air and many bird and animal species are threatened with extinction. So eat, drink and be merry for tomorrow you may be dead!

So the poem 'Cod War' is a tongue in cheek look at the revenge of nature. Is that what we might deserve?

Finally I deal with mental illness. Peoples lives can be ravaged by mental exhaustion, distress or other reactive malfunctions of the mind. Mental illnesses involving 'psychotic episodes' such as schizophrenia and bipolar disorder can contribute to symptoms considered by onlookers as forms of 'madness'.

Unemployment, relationship breakdowns and the grief of death can all lead to episodes of depression, anxiety and alcohol or substance abuse. My poem 'The Tramp' will perhaps provide some enlightenment to mental conditions that people too often misunderstand and misinterpret. Some people have genuine contempt for people with mental health problems which is rather sad bordering on pathetic.

£ $ €

MONEY

The money was on the table
the cheque is in the post
the credit is due for payment
who is paid the most?

The interest was too expensive
the money is in the banks
the government spent far too much
on weaponry and tanks.

The amount spent on education
the sums for hospital attention
the bills for public transport
the cost of retirement pension.

The tax paid, the bonuses awarded
the stipends and the fees
the credit and loans outstanding
the excessive outlay on spending sprees.

The wages, the salaries
the sums which have been agreed
the repossession of the houses
the absurdity of greed.

The rich man, the poor man
the living beyond the means
the best designer clothing
the holey pair of jeans.

Money makes the world go round
it lubricates the trade
it has become a big obsession
for the grossly overpaid.

David Wilding 6-2-09

MASTERS OF THE UNIVERSE

We are the masters of the universe
we like to make lots of money
our greed is obscene and perverse
but we think it's rather funny.
We've made your economy go bust
but we've made ourselves very rich
after all one day we're just ashes and dust
Isn't life just a bitch!
So if you're going to moan and complain
we're not prepared to listen.
So what, the economy's down the drain?
But gold, our aim, doth glisten.
Not only that,
we think you're rather stupid,
and some of you are far too fat,
maybe you see our attitude as putrid.
You're to blame, because you let us proceed,
you were busy working and living life,
to notice our excessive greed,
now there's nowt but trouble and strife,
and our hearts will not concede.
The environment is of no concern,
our policy is 'slash and burn',
and when this world is totally exhausted,
we won't worry what we've extorted.
Because we are masters of the universe,
we don't agree our greed is perverse.

THE GREEDY MAN

The greedy man,
ignores the wishes of the needy man,
he speculates and accumulates,
as in business affairs he participates.
Worldly goods are his prime motive,
paintings, antiques, boats and things automotive.
To his friends he likes to demonstrate,
his fantastic ability to accumulate.
A private plane, a couple of houses,
his wife has many shoes and additional blouses.
Five star hotels, executive meetings,
champagne and caviar, expensive greetings,
expense accounts and business lunches,
tax exemptions and playing hunches.
So let's ask him, "are you really happy?"
his reply will be very snappy,
"Unless you have more,
life would be a bore,
without an aim,
of financial gain,
life would be too much of a pain."
So he'll continue to ignore,
the disadvantaged and the poor,
and to rant and to rave,
of the need to save.
But where in all of this,
is the creation of bliss?
When all of the time,
poverty and crime,
murder, rape and mental disintegration,
threatens the safety and sanity of the nation?
So spare a thought of spiritual need,
if you are absorbed in a cycle of greed.

COD WAR

Cod crawled out of the ocean
They colonised the land
they lay in wait at the dead of night
and crawled along the sand.
They grabbed men and women too,
And threw them into the sea
Where they became fish instead
None were able to flee
Then the cod began to fish for men
They fished them to extinction
It's what men would have done instead,
Only with less distinction.
All the birds of the air did sing
All the animals did rejoice
For the cod who colonised the land
Were less cruel and harsh of voice
And if the cod had not done this
If they had stayed in the ocean deep
Man would have extinguished everything
Because to him all else was cheap.
Even those of piety, even those of faith,
Regard the world that we dominate
As subject to our whim
So think of what we do today,
before it's just too late.

THE TRAMP

David Wilding

Shuffling along,
hair all dirty,
shoes falling apart,
the homeless man strokes his beard.
Grubby fingers, holey pants,
greasy jacket, face in a trance.
Bending over the litter bin,
picking out a rusty tin.
"Spare the price of a cuppa, guv?"
lacking faith, warmth and love.
Broken by the pressure of life,
hurt by hatred and divorced from wife.
Reviled and spat on by tormenting kids,
shielding tears from heavy eyelids.
Rejected by the employment game,
shuffling along, in mental pain.
Under the pier,
a place for the night,
beaten up by a youth in a fight.
Well-heeled passer by,
looks down his nose, averts his eye.
Cut and broken,
bleeding and lame,
shouts like a madman,
not caring of shame.

Settling down in cardboard box,
smelly feet and dirty socks.
Shuffling along in the wind and the rain,
face contorted with mental pain.
Buys a bottle,
takes a drink,
drunken oblivion,
lets him think,
of times gone by, of better days,
of living at home,
of children to raise.
Cut off by all he used to love,
separated, broken,
sometimes mad,
rejected as a hopeless dad.
Death awaits, a blessed relief,
or prison,
branded as a thief.
Shuffling along,
to who knows where,
lacking faith, lacking care.

DECLARATION OF INTENT AND FAITH

Surely as a "Christian" society we should be concerned for the welfare of people such as 'The Tramp, and some are, but not all, including a very significant number of self-satisfied "I've booked my passport to eternity and have to do nothing else" religious adherents. Some care hardly at all other than for the making of more money. Jesus Himself said that it would be difficult to render to God appropriately if you also worship money.

As for Muslims, Jews, Hindus, atheists and Manchester United supporters; well we all have our 'sins', do we not?

Yes, I too have my sins, although in theory Jesus had none. None I say, none whatsoever.

Let He who is without sin assume the role of Jesus and watch as the hypocrites crucify Him!

I will admit here and now:
    I admire Jesus, and,
        I love Him as a brother
            and fellow human being,
                and as a 'Saviour'.

Some people might see me as a 'prophet', others perhaps as a dead loss!

I see myself very clearly: Someone who wants positivity to outweigh, outwit and outplay negativity. I want people to thrive, not to wither and die.

If I am a prophet; a prophet of what? of doom, of hope, of redemption?

My short story, 'The Prophet' does illustrate how difficult the role might be.

To be or not to be.
That is the question.

And the answer must surely be:
    Who cares?

Who cares?
I think I care,
I care for the future,
I care for the plight of the innocent,
I even care for the plight of the guilty.
Yet I care little for those who care only for themselves.

>Because caring
>involves sharing
>and living
>means giving
>something of yourself.

THE PROPHET

In those days the darkness was very dark. Then someone switched a light on and it was not so dark.

A man came from the east.

Many more come from the east but none from the west. A small number came from the north and about twenty from the south, but none from the west.

The Supreme Leader, also called 'Mr. Bean' by the man from the Cable Company, said he would set up an independent, biased, committee of inquiry to find out why no men came from the west.

And the man who had come from the east, a man called Jonah, did say unto the others excluding those who had not come from the west, "Verilly I say unto you, these are dark days indeed and we as a group of people must lighten the darkness."

Then he went off and hid in a cave.

The men from many quarters, except the west, gathered in small groups and muttered amongst themselves, "What does this mean. How can we lighten the darkness?" and then they said amongst themselves, "I'm hungry. Let us go forth and seek nutritious sustenance."

Nine days later, when the man called Jonah had emerged from the cave, people had gathered in the village square and they did see the man and they said unto him, "What didst thou mean when thou sayeth 'let us lighten the darkness'?"

The man called Jonah did reply, "the darkness is vast and all consuming. We must not let the darkness prevail."

Then the man said, "I'm now going into the Fox and Ferret for a ploughmans and a pint. I shall speak more unto you when I have drunk of the golden bitter."

Some of the men attempted to follow the man into the pub, but he said unto them, "Bother me not. I require time to formulate a plot."

They dispersed, muttering, "Why doesn't he clarify the meaning of his words?"

The man emerged from the pub an hour and a half later.

"There he is. Let's ask him," said one of the villagers, and a small number of people approached the man.

"What do you mean about the darkness. Are you a prophet. Do you know things which are important. Where have you come from. Are you married. Are you a religious man?" various people asked.

"The darkness will not prevail if you resist it. You must seek the light. I have come so that you may see the darkness as a threat and so that you may walk in the light," said the man.

"Is he drunk do you think?" someone asked.

"I don't think he makes sense, perhaps he's mad," said another.

"No, let's listen, he may have knowledge. Perhaps he is a prophet," said a youngish man.

"He's talking nonsense, let's ignore him. Go away and get a proper job," said Billy Bigot, almost shouting.

The man walked away from the people saying, "I shall say nothing else if you are against my words. I shall go somewhere else. I am not drunk I have only had 2 pints. My wife has left me. I am not a fascist, I am a man of peace. I know of God but I have no religion."

"He's crazy," said some

"He's a genius," said others

"He's drunk," said a few

"I think he's quite cute," said a love struck teenage girl.

"I don't like the way he dresses," said a fashion-conscious young lady.

"Let's happy slap him," said a teenage dropout boy.

But the man walked away from the people and went to the bus station and caught a bus to the town further along the valley.

The people of the village forgot about the man apart from a small group who remembered his words and sought to conquer the darkness, even though they were not sure why the darkness was a threat. And for some the light prevailed but for others the darkness consumed them but very few understood that the prophecy was true.

The man got off the bus in the town further along the valley and once again some listened while others were scornful.

Then the man just disappeared, and people did not know where he disappeared to, but some remembered his words and were changed by what he said. Even though the darkness prevailed in many cases, the light prevented the death of many and many came to know the advantages of a life lived in the pursuit of justice, truth and light.

What became of the prophet you may ask. Prophets come and prophets go but the message hardly ever alters, unless the prophet alters the message. Sometimes the message may not be a true message. How can we ever know, other than by seeking wisdom for ourselves and by recognising the truth.

The day of redemption was yesterday, is today and will be tomorrow. To hate is to surrender to darkness, although sometimes it is hard to love and to tolerate because the darkness can be vast and all consuming.

MAY YOU . . .

May your eyes seek out the virtue in others

may you have compassion and tolerance for those who are different and those we don't understand

may your days of darkness and woe be illuminated with the light of hope

may your troubles be comforted and may their resolution strengthen your faith

may your enemies be reconciled to you and may they see that your wisdom prevails

may your pain and grief be eclipsed by your days of joy

may your faith never be arrogant and pompous

may your confidence be matched by humility

may your life be blessed with purpose and meaning

may you walk through the gates of eternity with Jesus as your guide.

David Wilding
January 2003

PROPHECY.

What does the future hold in store,
will there be peace, will there be war?
Will God punish the conflict creators,
will there be termination for the justice haters?
Will time reach a turning point,
a discontinuity, a curve or a joint?
A new heaven and a new earth,
a paradise of plenty, never a dearth?
Who will be saved and who will be lost,
what is the price, the consideration, the cost?
Will there be a Judgement Day,
a time in which the guilty pay?
And where to then, to earth or to heaven,
will there be battle at Armageddon?
The prophets have told us conflicting stories,
of justice from God and angelic juries.
We don't really know and we shouldn't worry,
and no-one's looking to find out in a hurry!

THE MYSTERY.

Out of chaos God created order,
Stars, planets, atmospheres and a border,
So why, you ask, does God allow,
earthquake, flood and sunken dhow?
It's a miracle that earth is even so stable,
so criticise not, for if He were able,
He would have made this earth more secure,
a consideration we should not ignore.
In creation God may have been fallible,
but in love, He is more capable.
But you still ask, what about dying,
where's the sense in all of our trying,
to improve and refine our methods of living,
if in the end it's so unforgiving?
O ye of little faith!
Those who die in innocence,
those who die in love,
those who die in the faith of Christ,
have a place in heaven above.
Where's heaven you ask,
where's your God of love,
where's your evidence,
of some sort of recompense?
So Mr. Clever human being,
you want to know everything,
you want to know of death,
is there an afterlife,
a hidden, phantom, breath?
That's the mystery,
the one that God won't tell,
life and death his only card,
now we don't believe in hell.

WHO ARE YOU TO JUDGE?

You would think that religion would generate compromise and compassion and sometimes it does but often it does not. In fact it creates judgmental bigots all too frequently.

People who will say things like, "There will be a day of judgment and those who did not know Jesus will suffer eternal punishment." (*) Hmm, that's not a nice God, that's a God who sends down fire and brimstone every time someone has a sexual inclination. A petulant God, created in the image of petulant religious people who think that 'sin' is something that someone else does, and who think that theirs is compensated for by: Jesus: and their sin is therefore not relevant.

(* How sad that people would wish such things on others because their failings and weaknesses are so ill-comprehended.)

But every cloud has a silver living and perhaps Jesus really has paved a road to eternity, but a road for whom?

Is a good, peacemaking Muslim better placed to enter the 'kingdom of heaven' than a bad, belligerent "Christian?"

On the issue of private lives many religious people are excessively judgmental. The sex as 'sin' brigade have a mindless, almost prurient, attitude towards the 'mistakes' others make in their private lives. Is this not a form of smugness? Good luck if you happened to marry the right person and have stayed faithful throughout your lives. Admittedly some people have private lives which are a mess because of selfishness and vanity. Stable marriages do nurture children with a more balanced outlook but it's amazing how many single parents bring-up children with a positive outlook too.

Because people take their religious beliefs and practices seriously, believing them to be important, this opens the door of conflict. Jesus believed by some to be 'God made man' or Muhammad, God's ultimate 'messenger'. But both, if alive today, would surely want their followers to be 'peacemakers', or is that just me being silly?

A 'Religious Gathering' illustrates the nature of the 'Beast'.

'The Moral Maze' which follows deals with the thorny question, "Is it easier for a homosexual to enter the kingdom of heaven than for a rich man?"

Does God reserve entry to the 'kingdom of heaven' only to practising Catholics perhaps? Or Protestants? Or Baptists? Or Muslims?

Surely only Jehovah's Witnesses can enter paradise.

Personally I think that only Buddhists who dress in green can enter the kingdom of heaven.

Would I want to go to a place where the earthly arguments go on into eternity? Perhaps God is very choosy and prefers attractive women, regardless of religious affiliation. Would a male to female transsexual quality too?

Poor old God, whatever criteria He opts for, someone isn't going to approve!

A RELIGIOUS GATHERING.

It was a Thursday morning, there was a knock on the door. It was Joseph and Jenny the Jehovah's Witnesses, "Don't you think that with all the evil in the world there is need for the help of God?" Standard opening lines, I thought.

I invited them in. Another knock, Jacob the Jew. Then another, Catherine the Catholic, and another, Mustaffa the Muslim.

And still they came: Millicent the Methodist, Egbert the Evangelical, Horatio the Hindu, Belinda the Buddhist, Bruce the Baptist, Melvin the Methodist, Maurice the Mormon, Arnold the atheist, Agnes the agnostic.

All either worshippers or indifferent to Yahweh/Jehovah, the God of love.

"But you Jehovah's Witnesses have got in all wrong," asserted Egbert.

"No, no," stated Mustaffa, "it is all of you Christians who are wrong. You Christians say that Jesus was the Son of God, and that Mary was the mother of God. How can that be so?? God has no mother or son. God is one."

Jacob cut in, "You're all wrong, only the Jews are the chosen people and our Messiah is yet to come."

Nathan was an unorthodox Jew and he now interrupted, "But you, Jacob, say that the Torah was dictated by God to Moses on Mount Sinai, whereas we believe it was written in different stages."

"Tosh and nonsense," retorted Jacob.

"But we believe that only we follow the true path," argued Joseph, "only we will survive Armageddon."

Arnold the atheist now made his point, "All of your religions are based on myth and nonsense, how can there be a God with all that power, when evil is allowed to prevail?"

The arguments started to become heated, the language more vitriolic. Fighting broke out.

I levitated in the corner of the room and shimmering in light staged a transfiguration. They were all so busy knocking seven bells out of each other that they missed it. I resumed normal bodily state and became tired of all the bickering.

I cut across the babble, "I thought that those of you who believe in God believed in a God of love, yet look at you fighting like cats and dogs over tiny differences in dogma and interpretation when everything you believe is based on uncertain historical evidence. Fine examples of a God of love aren't you? Now get out and leave me alone!"

They filed out of the house muttering, "Raving nutter if you ask me."

So much for their witnessing to a God of love, and thereafter I declared my house a "religion free zone."

But there is a God, although why He should accept petty zealots into His Realm is something He will have to decide.

THE MORAL MAZE

Michael Buerk: Today's question on the moral maze is, 'Is it easier for a rich man to enter the kingdom of heaven than a poofter?' Archbishop Twit, what do you think?

Archbish Twit: Well I would have to say that Jesus was not fond of rich people but was rather ambiguous concerning poofters. The question also needs to be asked, 'Is the poofter a practising poofter or not and just how rich is the rich man?'

> Personally I think that the rich man cannot enter the kingdom of heaven but the poofter has a strong chance as long as he's not too much of a poofter.

Michael Buerk: And Archbishop Bigot how do you see it?

Archbish Bigot: I think it is quite clear from Biblical text that the poofter has no chance of entering the kingdom of heaven but the rich man has a very strong chance because he will have utilised his talents in accordance with Jesus's parable of the talents. This, however, seems to clash with Jesus's story of the camel and the eye of the needle; and as the Most Reverend Twit muses: "Just how rich is the rich man?'

David Starkey: I must interrupt at this point to strongly disagree with the Reverend Bigot, who is almost certainly a bigot because of what he has said. Poofters or gay people as I prefer to refer to them as, can most definitely enter the kingdom of heaven because we are created in the image of God and therefore my God is also gay and it would be absurd for Him in His supreme wisdom to discriminate against people who are just like He is.

Archbish Bigot: Mr. Starkey is most definitely wrong. How can God be a poofter? God is as straight as they make them. No, I stand by my assertion that poofters have no chance of eternal life.

Archbish Twit: No, I must disagree with the learned Reverend and side with Mr. Starkey, although his assertion that god is a poofter too is clearly patently absurd. I repeat what I said earlier, 'If the poofter is only a bit poofterish' – he clearly has a strong chance.

Michael Buerk: There does seem to be a difference of opinion between the two Archbishops, but David, what about the rich man; can he also enter the kingdom of heaven?

David Starkey: Well of course he can. Archbishop Bigot is right to say that those who utilise their talents to the full and make loads of money are truly worthy in the sight of God the gay.

Michael Buerk: Bishop Bigot you pose the question of just how rich the rich man can be. Can you be more specific, can a man be too rich to enter the kingdom of heaven?

Archbish Bigot: I'm an Archbishop not just an ordinary Bishop Michael, if you please. You are right to ask, 'How rich is too rich?' Perhaps the billionaire is too rich but the millionaire is almost certainly not.

Archbis Twit: I would like to come in at this point. I believe that even a million pounds is too rich but clearly a million U.S. dollars is not. I firmly believe that through meditation and prayer that God has told me that £999,999.98 pence is the limit, one penny more and you're excluded.

David Starkey: I cannot agree with such arbitrary figures. What about the effects of inflation? God surely salutes and rewards efforts to generate prosperity and wealth whereas the poor are feckless and lazy.

Michael Buerk: Ah, welcome Professor von Hairdryer. Were you delayed in the traffic? Professor von Hairdryer as you will know is the author of the book, "The Road to Syphillis." Professor can you shed light on just how rich someone would be to be excluded?

Prof. von Hairdryer: Yes, indeed, the Archbishop asserts that a million pounds is too much, but values are relative and as Mr. Starkey correctly states, inflation distorts values, but one thing is quite clear, a rich man with either syphillis or A.I.D.S., especially if he is a poofter will definitely not enter the kingdom of heaven. But in terms of absolute wealth, the figure must approximate to £10 million, although one can never be certain because no one can truly know the mind of God.

Archbis Twit: I can!

Michael Buerk: Well Archbishop Twit clearly believes that rich people cannot enter the kingdom of heaven, but as for poofters, well who knows, and who really cares? On next weeks' moral maze we discuss whether sex before marriage is a sin too far. Thank you gentlemen and poofters for your contributions to todays' debate. now I'm off to spend a few thousand pounds to get below the threshold and be on the safe side.

GOOD, EVIL AND SATAN

We are spiritual beings with souls. Some people have an incredible capacity to be kind, generous, tolerant and loving. But we are all different, very different. Some people can be intolerant, rude, selfish and full of hatred. What makes us what we are?

Well as a starting point it's our brains, and people have different brains. The brain gives us our minds and our nervous systems. We inherit characteristics from our parents, yet our brothers and sisters can be very different from us. The brain also determines our sexual characteristics and inclinations.

Inside our brains our minds contain our memories, our thoughts, our attitudes. Our intelligence and our aptitudes are also functions of our minds. Physical characteristics may influence the functioning of our minds too. The person with good looks and physical attractiveness may be vain and egotistical particularly if they have an interesting personality. The less attractive may be more reticent and cautious.

Education, experiences, social status, access to wealth and resources, physical and mental skills all make up the contributing factors determining our personalities and attitudes.

The person who has been bullied may become withdrawn or they may develop a thick skin and adopt a bullying personality themselves, as a defence mechanism. Those of generous spirit may be taken advantage of, and learning the lesson may adopt a meaner attitude at a later stage of life.

Our personalities can change over time. Living in an environment in which conflict is frequent is likely to make us more belligerent. We can rise above our circumstances through sheer willpower and determination. There are many stories of reformed criminals who go on to do amazing things to reform and assist others who are struggling with life.

We also react differently to stress. Some people thrive on a moderate amount of stress. It can serve as a stimulant. Other people have very low levels of tolerance to stress, sometimes developing mental foibles as a consequence.

But what makes a person 'good' or 'evil'. Firstly I must emphasise that some people have little or no control over certain mental manifestations because they are mentally ill or damaged in some way. It is premeditation which determines whether a person can be said to be good or evil. Some people plan a course of action to give gratification from causing harm to others. Others try to practise strategies which contribute towards the welfare and physical or mental comfort of those they have contact with. Some people just don't think things through and their actions can be thoughtless rather than malicious.

As for the mentally ill schizophrenic who, for example, hears the voice of 'John the Baptist' telling him to kill someone, could they be said to be an agent of 'Satan'? Of course not! Mental illness is better understood but there is still a lot of superstitious ignorance surrounding it.

If one believes in a 'force for good', call it God, then it is equally possible that there is a 'force for evil', which we might call Satan. But how do those forces operate and can they influence the course of events?

Jehovah's Witnesses saw the two World Wars of the 20th Century as indicative of the presence of Satan at work in the world. The Holocaust and the cruelty of the Nazi regime in Germany seems to indicate a depth of evil in the human spirit which is generally dormant in times of prosperity and peace but war brutalises people who go on to commit acts of almost mindless bestiality when viewed from a more tranquil age. How on earth could someone contemplate the hanging of a child at Auschwitz as a symbol of the apparent worthlessness of another group of human beings? No, that's not Satan, it's just downright evil.

So I will have to confess to not understanding what Satan might be. Yet when people treat other people with such contempt that they seem to gain some satisfaction from their suffering it seems to be reasonable to believe that they must be 'out of their minds' with evil intent, yet apparently in control of their reasoning and not 'mentally ill.' It is also credible to think of such arrogance and evil as being 'Antichrist' in that it puts itself at variance with the teachings of those such as Jesus Christ who see a better way of thinking and behaving.

What follows is some of the thoughts generated on this difficult aspect of the human spirit. Can Satan use evil to unleash appalling behaviour in the human domain or are some people just bad people?

Perhaps Adolf Hitler was a very specific 'Antichrist' or perhaps antichrist comes in many different guises when things go badly wrong in human activities.

I do not hold with the idea of specific 'satanic' possession but prejudice, contempt and hatred when premeditated does often lead to evil actions.

Mr. Hitler was one of my earliest poems. There follows a meditation on the nature of 'Satan' and a poem 'Things Satanic': With respect to the 'unnecessary abortion' line, I think it is unfortunate that such things happen but would not wish to demonise a woman's right to choose. Psychologically it must be a hard decision to make.

There follows an essay reflecting on the confusion and turmoil which unravelled in Europe in the 20th Century. War brutalises, yet genuine bravery and acts of compassion still happen right in the 'eye of the storm.'

In conclusion, we are an amalgam of dark thoughts and ideas and yet capable of higher order thinking. Such is the human spirit.

The final poem in this section is 'Just Desserts' written after a suicide bombing in Lahore, Pakistan. Does God give us our just desserts, if or as and when we come to be judged for our earthly endeavours?

MR. HITLER

Mr. Hitler was an anti-Christ,
because hatred and fear was his main device,
to subdue, coerce and marshall his people,
into a nation of sickness and evil.
What kind of man legalises elimination,
of women and children of God's creation?
What kind of man tortures and revels,
in killing and letting troops work as devils?
I'll answer this question,
with a simple suggestion,
Mr. Hitler was no man at all,
no not even one with only one ball.
I wouldn't even consider this thing of a creature,
when visiting God would even feature,
on a list for reincarnation,
as a frog, an ant or a lump of bacon,
because man who plays God,
is distinctly odd,
unless he prays for guidance,
in a spirit of kindness,
and even then,
he should think again,
and ask all his brothers,
and sometimes their mothers,
is this right or is it wrong,
should I put it in song?
Perhaps Hitler was really King Kong!

SATAN

Some Christian fundamentalists have got themselves in a terrible tangle on this aspect. They see Satan as an external "spirit" able to possess those who reject "Christian values."

They have been brainwashed by films like the "Exorcist" and the "Omen" into believing that satanic possession and the anti-Christ are realities, and that the anti-Christ will come before the "final conflict."

It is quite easy to see why some people believe in the concept of "possession", but it is a concept borne out of fear and superstition rather than rational analysis. In the past people whose behaviour was awkward and bizarre were labelled "mentally ill" and they were institutionalized partly out of fear, partly out of embarrassment. It is sometimes hard to understand why some people behave strangely or commit ghastly acts against other people, but it is a weakness of the human spirit and mind, not a consequence of an external "force for evil."

In the past people who were mocked and abused sometimes lapsed into retaliation by "putting a curse" on their abusers. Understandably, this can be disconcerting, but to put the label "witch or wizard" and to imprison, torture or kill them, had more to do with the psychological weaknesses of their persecutors than the fault of the victim.

The modern church still retains a fanatical element who see the hand of Satan in certain forms of behaviour. Rock music, promiscuity and drugs are often seen as "Satanic." The myth of ritual "satanic abuse" has grown and modern persecutors have subjected innocent parents to horrific allegations.

Abuse in any form is a dreadful failing of the human spirit but to create a superstitious aura about it hinders logical investigation and analysis.

I see the "satanic spirits" as being failings of the human spirit. In fact, they could be said to be defiance of God's Law, incorporated in the Ten Commandments. These "seven spirits" have been distilled into the "seven deadly sins" by some commentators.

It is easy to see them as being aspects of "possession." Those who are possessed by the human weaknesses of jealousy, greed, pride, covetousness, hatred, lust and sloth, frequently appear to be "possessed" by their weaknesses.

As for the imminent arrival of "Satan's Son," cryptically described by the code 666, to start the "final conflict," such an idea would be laughable were it not for the fact that it is a psychological reality to some fanatics.

This century has seen acts of dreadful wickedness perpetrated by people and leaders who believe in the "survival of the fittest," "superior races," and other wholly abhorrent ideology.

Satan can be YOU if you reject good and accept evil ways of thought and behaviour.

THINGS SATANIC

Malicious gossip, evil thought,
plotting against a man who won't be bought,
manipulation and thought distortion,
domination and unnecessary abortion.
These are things inspired by evil,
invading the mind like a hungry weevil.
Ugly buildings rapidly erected,
necessary resources misdirected.
Profiting from another's misery,
exploitation wages and forms of slavery.
Greed, domination and power abuse,
unnecessary authority and its misuse
Torture, mugging, murder, rape,
beating someone as a jolly jape.
Pushing drugs, corrupting youth,
language and behaviour uncouth.
Things satanic are inspired by hatred,
lust and greed, jealousy unabated.
They should be obvious to those who search,
to those who moralise and go to church.
Beatles records and cuddly toys,
harmless fun, girls with boys.
Let's not attach evil intent,
to normal behaviour, clean not bent.
For God put us here to savour enjoyment,
without harming others in our employment.

THE 20TH CENTURY. SATAN'S VICTORY & THE BIRTH OF THE NEW AGE

For 1,500 years religion was the truth. Of course that truth was questioned by dissenters and schisms occurred. Then science, knowledge and information not only challenged that truth but produced new truths.

A flat earth at the centre of the Universe became a sphere orbiting a star. The world was a bigger place, the Universe was a mystery.

It had all been so certain, in some respects reassuring. God made everything in 7 days. Jesus told us about life after death and the Kingdom of Heaven. Hell was the consequence of sin. Adam and Eve were uniquely human, not animal, created not evolved.

Religion was still the truth but new truths modified the old truth.

Scientific discoveries allowed new thinking to take place. Information was more widely disseminated. Newspapers told the truth. Political leaders knew about the issues and guided opinion. The church backed the politicians when it could be clearly seen that their stance was just. There was justice in war, the church told one set of leaders, who fought another set of leaders who were also fighting a just war. Justice could be apportioned by authority, particularly as the church nearly always agreed.

But the old certainties began to crumble. Fossil evidence suggested that man was an animal. Darwin indicated that man had evolved. We were ape men. Of course we are not, said conservatives, the ape men died out, we were created by God as the finished product.

The voice of authority was flawed but many were too ill informed or ill educated to recognise it. People began to clamour for democracy; aristocratic regimes had to surrender some of their powers. Industrialisation brought about urbanisation, new methods of living and new forms of thinking.

Economics and Empire building guided policy. National self-interest legitimised actions. Monarchies felt threatened by new ideas. New weapons of war and mass armies changed the face of conflict.

Thus dawned the 20th Century, a new age of hope but an age of uncertainty. Population grew. New ideas were disseminated. Communication became more rapid. People still relied on leaders to provide the ideas, opinions and guidance.

Armed struggle was right. It was necessary to show strength when agreement broke down. Attack or be attacked.

So in 1914 when Europe erupted into conflict it was the right thing to do to enlist and to do your duty. God would be on the side of the just and a just death was better than surrender.

Then the peace. The age of paper money had arrived. Gold had served it's purpose. The value of money became a less certain thing. The world failed to recognise the power of economics and the uncertainty of politics. Information was more widely available but panic and superstition still prevailed because there wasn't enough information. How could people understand a new system in a new world? History hadn't enough experience. Economics hadn't enough ideas. Change was too rapid. Invention was delivering new technology, new industry, new products. It was a new age.

Old certainties crumbled. Religion was marginalised. Politics and economics indicated that self-interest should prevail. Man had evolved from an ape man. Adam and Eve was a myth. God might not even exist.

Into this intellectual vacuum entered nihilism. New thinking was needed. Old truths were myths. The rock of religion as truth was crumbling

Economic collapse. Nationalism. Germany the crushed and defeated and unfairly treated. Russia, in turmoil. Strong solutions were needed and there was no place for opposition and challenge.

The strong leadership would explain their thinking and the reasons why their ideas were correct through new methods of communication. People listened and most believed. Common aims and objectives meant that dissenters were troublemakers. Scapegoats became easy targets.

In Britain and America democracy had deep roots. It's philosophical justification was well understood.

Christianity stood in the way of the strong leaders. It bowed and accepted second place to political necessity. In the Communist states it was crushed. In the Fascist states it was allowed to survive as long as it's dissenting voice was not raised.

In Germany Hitler felt that politics needed to assume religious authority. The leadership needed obedience and sometimes worship. Only the strong would survive in this brave new world. The weak link must become strong or be removed. Compassion was weakness. The people were brainwashed into a belief in the national will.

Religion had left a vacuum. It's truths were no longer truths but conjecture. Into that vacuum Hitler ruthlessly dragged superstitions, half-truths, paganistic ritual and belief, and any thinking which confirmed German supremacy.

Is it any wonder that when Christianity is so comprehensively subdued that one of the most inhumane regimes in human history takes its place?

From this period of turmoil and change in which certainties became uncertainties came horrific conflict, horrific atrocities and the weapons of mass destruction.

-Then from an age of uncertainty new seeds of hope. New knowledge. Better information and education. A resurrection of old philosophies to sweep aside the tide of superstition and false ideology.

In this new age people are free to decide for themselves. Better communications and more leisure time allows people to seek information and evidence and to make informed choices.

However, in this age of questioning there are new uncertainties. Leaders who disseminated the received truth are no longer believed with absolute certainty.

Religion is just a possible truth of many differing possibilities. In particular its stance on time, space and eternity is seriously suspect. The spiritual vacuum in human psychology is there; can the Christian religion preserve some of its old truths while adapting to some of the new truths? If it cannot its power to influence will continue to wane. Atheistic cosmological explanations of our place in space and time will effectively become the religion of the age.

The New Age is here. The rock of faith laid down by Jesus needs restoration.

θ

JUST DESSERTS

Shi'a and sunni
sometimes it 's quite funny.
But death in Lahore
is 'faith' very poor.
Muslim and Jew
death occurs there too.
Why can't we live,
Why can't we forgive?
I've decided my belief
should never give grief.
I've decided my God,
should never be odd.
So let me declare
of a faith so rare.
I believe what you receive,
isn't determined by what you perceive
and regardless of what you believe.
But that you get just desserts,
and sometimes that hurts.

TIME GENTLEMEN (AND LADIES) PLEASE

As sentient beings we seek to understand our place in space and time. Where have we come from and where are we going?

The coming and the going of the seasons. What causes the sun to come up in the mornings and to go down at night. Ancient peoples wondered what might happen if the sun failed to rise again the next day. The 'sun god' was the most important of the 'gods' because without the sun we would almost certainly perish.

People have always speculated about the 'end of time.' What happens then? Naturally this speculation links in to religious thinking. If there is a God or there are 'gods' does He or they control our ultimate destinies in terms of our time here on earth and our possible destiny beyond death. Heavy stuff!

Jesus Christ Himself speculated on what the future might hold. He envisaged the coming of the Kingdom of God and there has been much speculation in religious circles ever since about what He meant and when it might happen. We even date our calendars from the time Jesus was supposed to have been born, although most religious historians think that the dating was inaccurate and He was born in 4 B.C.

When bad things happen in the world some people begin to see events portending the 'end of time' or the world. The Black Death of 1348-1349 in Europe was God's punishment upon the world and 'end of time' hysteria predominated.

In recent years I have read a lot of books on British, European and world history and it is fascinating to imagine the lives, motivations and thoughts of people of times past. Ian Mortimer takes us on a journey into the medieval mind in 'The Time Traveller's Guide to Medieval England.' C.J. Sansom allows us to imagine the Tudor age in his historical novels set in the time of Henry VIII.

What was life like in the late Georgian, early Victorian era? The industrial revolution, the age of steam. The railway-building mania of the 1840s.

The good times and the bad times. The wretched lives of some, the privileged lives of others. The wasted lives cut short by wars, disease and famine.

And what of our times. What might happen in the immediate future? Should we be optimistic or pessimistic? Should we live for the moment or plan for the future?

Old Father Time keeps rolling along and we are carried along in its wake.

Will the world ever end and what happens then? The Daily Nonsense (End of the World edition) clearly got its 'facts' wrong as the universe did not come to an end at the end of March 2009, so the soothsayers will have to think again.

There follows an essay 'End of Time(ism)' written when I was well into my 'God phase', when I was trying to make sense of world events. People talk of an expanding universe which will get cooler or collapse on itself, the 'Big Crunch'. Although our understanding of time is far superior than it was 2,000 years ago, we still don't know what happens next, and perhaps it is better that we don't!

The poem 'Reignition' is a speculation on what might happen after the 'end'; a new beginning perhaps?

Three more poems follow on the time theme: 'I Might Have Been', 'Passing By' and 'Days', followed by a silly description of the Incredibly Reverend Brian Twit's book, "Prepare for the Second Coming".

So there we are, time for a cup of tea and a biscuit!

For most of us the end of time is when we die, but then again maybe it's not, as the 'Angel of Death' poem suggests. If we are 'saved' by our religious faith surely we should have the correct faith? Back to the Buddhists dressed in green as the 'chosen ones' again. If God does judge us to be fit to live again in His universe surely He would select us by how we have lived not by how we practised our faith.

Who can ever know the mind of God except Mrs. Ethel Gumboil of Acacia Avenue, Accrington?

THE DAILY NONSENSE   90p   or free when the world ends

END OF THE WORLD EDITION BY OUR PSYCHOTIC REPORTER ANDREW ARMAGEDDON

NUTTER: End of the world campaigner, Rupert Nutter, has asserted that it is important for the world to end soon in order that the new world can be introduced. "This world is rubbish but the new world will be great," said Nutter yesterday. "I, of course, carry no blame for this world being rubbish, because I'm almost perfect."

END OF WORLD DELAYED
Jovial Witnesses last night became miserable witnesses as the predicted end of the world did not happen at 9.22 p.m. After waiting until 10.22, 11.22 and 12.22 a.m., they went home for a cup of cocoa and yet another reinterpretation of Biblical prophecy. A spokesman for the Morons said, "We knew they were wrong."

QUEEN TO CLOSE DOWN UNIVERSE
Her Majesty the Queen of the U.K. has been asked by God Enterprises to officiate at the closing ceremony of the universe. This will almost certainly happen at the end of March 2009.

The Daily Nonsense has accessed a copy of the Queen's address: "God Enterprises has decided to close down the universe after 18 billions magnificent years. The high cost of operating and maintaining a universe has precipitated this decision. The decision has largely been caused by greedy bankers not rendering unto God that which is God's. God bless you all and in the days not to come let us pray that there will come a day when there will be a new and improved universe."

END OF THE WORLD
Odds. When will the world end? Have your say with 'Mugbet'
3rd Jan. 2009 10/1
6th June 2009 8/1
4th March 2012 7/1
9th Dec. 2014 4/1

REPENT!
Mr. Sidney Spungeon, well-known predicter of things was seen, yes-

terday (Wednesday) bearing a placard, "repent the end of the week is nigh!" Amongst other accurate predictions, he forecast rain one Saturday afternoon and that Arsenal would lose a football match in 2008.

'Keep up the good work Sidney', says the Daily Nonsense.

END OF TIME (ISM).

We need to differentiate between a slide towards "dystopia", the survival of the species, and the "end of time".

Evangelical Christianity utilises the Biblical predictions concerning the "end of time". The Book of Revelation portends conflict at the end of time. Jesus, Himself, predicted a "second coming" at which time would end and souls would be split into two groups, one group going to heaven and the other group to hell. As David Jenkins, the Bishop of Durham, has, in my opinion, rightly said, Our God could not be so cruel as to subject the "failed souls" to eternal torture. yet to throw away the concept of "Divine retribution" is, in my opinion, extremely dangerous. There are already too many arrogant people on this planet who think they have a God-given right to judge others but that they will be immune, whatever the evidence to the contrary.

The Jehovah's Witnesses talk of the 'saved' and those who simply pass away. God certainly punishes disgraceful sins like those committed by corrupt abusers of power, but I prefer to believe that those souls spend a great deal of time in the "void" before being re-admitted to the realm of the living. Where? Somewhere in the Universe, on a particular planet, or perhaps the ultimate accolade, the "Kingdom of Heaven", as a result of an amazing life of devotion to the values and principles of God.

Perhaps the perpetrators of the Holocaust, are indeed terminated for ever. The Holy Spirit, and the Holy Spirit alone is the ultimate Judge and Jury. (Perhaps having taken evidence and advice from the "greats" like Jesus, Mohammed and Moses, Buddha and Mother Theresa of Calcutta might have an input into the process, I would not wish to offend the religious convictions of any grouping). The only group I would exclude are the intolerant religious zealots who create conflict, violence, war and death to others with their belligerence.

A slide into dystopia is seen by some as a portent of the end of time.

DYSTOPIA, in my opinion, IS NOT A GOD-INFLICTED OR SATAN-INFLICTED STATE. IT IS CAUSED BY HUMAN FAILINGS.

An environmental disaster resulting from mans' mismanagement of the planet would equally be self-imposed, but changes in the environment could also be caused by solar activity or a meteorite bombardment. Cosmologists see these as random possibilities. Evangelical Christians see these as acts of a wrathful God, portending the end of time.

Such activity would not actually be an "end to time" but a cosmological disaster. Time would still go on in other parts of the Universe. The Sun would still burn, so time would continue. Cosmologists postulate that the Sun will still burn as a viable star for about 5 billion years.

Hysteria concerning the "second coming" is frequent when a person who proclaims himself as "spiritually aware" gathers credibility and followers. But no person could ever be aware of the "end of time".

As the year 2000 is approached, superstition will be ignited again concerning the predictions of Nostrodamus and various others who have predicted that the "end of time" or the "second coming" is imminent.

I prefer to think that the prediction of a World Religion transcending conventional barriers of hatred and prejudice is a better prediction. Let's face it, the barriers between Islam, Christianity, Judaism, are nonsense since they all worship the God of Abraham, Isaac and Jacob. The human race needs to work across boundaries of prejudice to create a workable philosophy to tackle the problems of an increasingly overpopulated planet.

As for predictions, surely the most sensible statement in the Bible is in the Book of Ecclesiastes: 3:11 "God has made everything to suit its time; moreover he has given men a sense of time past and future, but no comprehension of God's work from beginning to end."

I believe that the size, structure and forces behind the Universe are inadequately understood for us to know whether time, structure and form will always exist. I do believe in a life-enhancing force behind the Universe which aims to propagate time. Whether the human spirit can be reproduced after death is still a mystery to me. I have faith that a life-enhancing spirit, call it God, exists.

Messiah and the end of time.

I have already detailed that "Christian psychology" is flawed, as it associates a Messiah with an end to time.

In his book "Judaism," Isidore Epstein explains the Messianic ideal from the perspective of the Jews. It is not concerned with the 'end of all things.' Messianic references throughout Hebrew prophecy point to an earthly future. The end aim of Messianism is to replace the present dominated by the senses; lust, greed, violence and passion, by a social order which through righteousness in knowledge and action creates a new earth and a new heaven.

WHO can know whether the Biblical record of Jesus as a major miracle-worker or even God-incarnate is accurate? The evidence is contained in books known as "the Gospels" handed down to us over the years. No person on earth today can know how much of the 'Jesus story' is fact, myth or a combination. It is surely more important how we live in the light of His teaching today. If there is an amazing era of miracles in the future, then let's just wait and watch!

RE-IGNITION

A barren and empty universe
in which all life is extinguished,
a chance to make another start
for those whose lives were distinguished.
The stars go out
the light disappears
the end has come
many billions of years.
The universe reloads
a massive ignition
stars begin to form
what an exhibition!
Perhaps such an event will not happen,
perhaps it all just conforms to a pattern.
Perhaps a God is behind it all,
perhaps we offended Him at the time of the fall.
All we can do is to live in faith and hope,
and maintain our love for humanity,
and heed words of wisdom to help us to cope.

David Wilding, 2005

I MIGHT HAVE BEEN

David Wilding: 2005

I might have never existed
I might never have been born
I might have been aborted
and not arrived on Saturday morn.
I might have come to earth in another kind of way.
Another person, another kind of animal
born in another body or form on that crucial day.
Perhaps by random chance I came to be born as me
or if not to my Mom and Dad,
to the couple at number three.
I might have been different from the man I am today
I might have been deformed, blind or made in a
                               different way.
Suppose I'd never had existed
never seen the earth so green
suppose my very fabric
had been reorganised as a runner bean.
We don't know how or why we were selected
to live a life as human
but I think that it's right to thank God
that He gave me chance to be a new man.
Maybe I've been here before
or maybe somewhere different
perhaps this is my only chance
to witness the world and see its way
and human kindness to advance.

PASSING BY

David Wilding: December 2004

I see them pass by the window,
some sauntering, some determined, some in a hurry.
On their way to make a rendevous,
some with optimism, some: faces furrowed with worry.
People passing by.
It's nearly Christmas,
people to meet, presents to buy.
Some come through the door,
time to stop for a drink, to meet for a chat,
"I said I'd meet her at four."
Some I recognise,
I know him, I recognise her,
I think I've met her, he looks familiar,
many I've probably passed many times,
some may be good, some guilty of crimes.
Some I may never see again.
Then my mind wanders,
I imagine people from the 60s, the 70s,
Some older, some gone.
Some new faces who weren't here then.
Many have passed, many pass through,
some I remember, some I never knew.
I'll pass by on another day,
someone else will watch me as I go on my way.
Passing through, passing by, passing on;
someone will see me, and then I'll just be gone.

DAYS

Sometimes there are days almost perfect,
sometimes there are days mostly abject,
sometimes people seem rude and angry,
sometimes everyone seems mostly friendly.
There are days and there are other days,
they change and they vary in innumerable ways.
The days of welcome and frequent laughter,
the days of tolerance and forgiveness thereafter.
Days of mourning and days of grief,
days of hope, sometimes too brief.
Days too short and days too long,
days of celebration and song.
The days we have cannot be measured,
there are days wasted and days to be treasured.
And when our days are finally at an end,
God may come, our souls to tend.

David Wilding
17th May 2008

"PREPARE FOR THE SECOND COMING"

a book of prophecy and revelation by the Incredibly Reverend Brian Twit, acclaimed author of the worst-selling, "Is the Fourth Horseman of the Apocalypse an Everton Supporter?"

In his new and revealing book, with a foreword by the Archbishop of Scunthorpe, the Reverend Twit under the influence of hallucinatory drugs and having applied the DaVinci Code, the Morse code, the Highway code and the Green Cross code to various passages in the Bible, is able to reveal that:

    i) the Anti-Christ is alive and living in Croydon,
    ii) Jesus was a Jew, (iii) Tesco sells beans,
    and makes the amazing predictions that:
    a) the next Pope will be a Catholic,
    b) the world will end at 4.30 p.m. on the 13th June, 2012.
    In addition, applying his amazing scholarship and by reading the tea leaves left behind after his early morning cup of P G Tips, the Reverend Twit also reveals that:
    i) Mrs Ethel Fang is, in fact, a man,
    ii) Jesus had a pet dinosaur called "Bonzo,"
    iii) The baby Jesus was wet-nursed by Tracy of Nazareth,
    iv) One of the wise men only had an I.Q. of 88.

"The Reverend Brian Twit applies a mixture of scholarship and insanity to produce this amazing analysis of Biblical mysteries." – Professor Ralph Bonkers, Oxford University.

"PREPARE FOR THE SECOND COMING" published by Nonsense Books is available from all bad booksellers priced £25.99. Or wait until it's sold in a discount bookstore for 99p in 12 months time.

THE ANGEL OF DEATH

And so I said to the angel of death,
"I seem to be short of breath."
He said, "The future looks bleak."
I said, "Yes, but I'm ever so meek."
He said, "Your end is near."
I said, "Can I have another beer"?
He said, "You seem to have no fear."
I said, "Does that seem ever so queer?"
He said, "You've got unbreakable faith,"
then said, "Perhaps you've got a pact with God?"
I said, "And many consider I'm very odd.
You see I've got faith in Christ the King."
"Oh no," he said, "you've a heavenly wing,
and the second will come when you're dead,
you're one of those who does my head.
I'll leave you alone for the time being,
and go and seek someone less capable of seeing!"

Fear not the angel of death but fear God, and fear your own prejudices and arrogance because God, although gracious and forgiving, has limits too.

***David** θ December, 2009*

AND NOW FOR SOMETHING COMPLETELY DIFFERENT!
THE COLOURS

What follows in the pages to come is a selection of some of the nonsensical short stories and poems wot I have wrote. The consumption of alcohol may have assisted the thinking process but I can assure you that no mind-altering drugs were involved.

The book finishes with a few 'Proverbs' which I conjured up and a concluding poem 'Jerusalem'.

Good luck on your journey through life. Perhaps we will meet again in a new heaven on a new earth.

Go in peace and hate no one unless they are selfish, prejudiced and arrogant but perhaps they deserve pity rather than hatred.

A NEW YEAR MESSAGE (2008) FROM:

THE INCREDIBLY REVEREND TARQUIN KIPPER-GERBIL GBH, HGV; ARCHBISHOP OF BOGTHORPE

Dear people wot are not as holy as wot I am, Here it is again, another year!

It doesn't seem to have been eight years since, on December 31st 1999 we waited with muted glee for the end of the world, and when it didn't happen, how sad we were.

It's hard to describe how holy I have been this year. I set fire to a sex shop. Bombed an abortionist clinic. And in one of my sermons stated quite clearly that poofters, single mothers and people who have sex outside of marriage are entirely to blame for global warming.

As for the poor misguided creature who named a toy bear 'Jesus', it was a blessing when we burnt her at the stake.

As I drive around in my large 'environmentally friendly' vehicle, I cannot but observe that people are far too greedy. Just because I have three houses, five cars, six holidays a year and a yacht in the Mediterranean, does not, however make me greedy because as one of the 'elect', mine is 'holy greed', whereas everyone else's greed is unholy greed. So stop it! Try a bit of self control!

The scurrilous rumour put about by 'Judas' (Rupert Branston-Chutney) concerning a secret liason between myself, your beloved Archbishop, and a lady of ill-repute, was quickly quashed and in addition we managed to prove him to be a wife-beater. Now that he has been excommunicated let us say a prayer for his soul, which will now burn in hell for the whole of eternity. How gracious is our God! Happy New Year and Shalom (sort of).

WE'RE ALL BONKERS NOW

The people of Upper Uppingham were of lower social status than the residents of Lower Uppingham who looked down on the Upper Uppinghamites. But of one thing, they were agreed, the people of Higher Smellingham were the lowest of the low, even though Higher Smellingham was on much higher ground. In fact, both Uppingham communities referred to the residents of Higher Smellingham as 'the smellies'.

The people of all three communities were concerned, however, when there was migration into their communities by people from Frequently Bonkingham, who had a terrible reputation for all manner of immorality. The 'bonkers' as they were sneeringly called, first moved into the cheaper properties in Higher Smellingham, where they became known as the 'smelly bonkers'. However, although the 'bonkers' had a dreadful reputation, they were tenacious and industrious, and in next to no time they were not only renting but purchasing properties in Upper Uppingham, hence becoming known as the 'Upper smelly bonkers'.

The residents of Lower Uppingham were scandalised shortly later when a 'bonker' actually had the effrontery to purchase a house in Lower Uppingham. The people of Upper Uppingham, never ones to miss a trick, decided it would be amusing to label all of the toffs of Lower Uppingham, 'smelly bonkers'. Lord Upper of Uppingham-in-the Vale issued a decree that no more smelly bonkers should purchase properties in Lower Uppingham. The upwardly mobile 'bonkers' sought legal advice and as the case progressed to the House of Lords, it was brought to the attention of the Queen, who ventured the comment, "It seems to me that they're all completely bonkers!"

And the matter was settled when the entire community was renamed "Higher, Lower Bonkingham".

FOOD, GLORIOUS FOOD!

David Wilding, December 2006

Is goats cheese, designed to please?
Should gateau be eaten in a bateau?
Is wine, of origin, divine?
Should tea be consumed at sea?
Is steak better than cake?
Does a whisky make you frisky?
Does Mandy enjoy a brandy?
Food and drink, it makes you think.
Should our food, be baked or stewed?
Would you like some cream, is that your dream?
Are chips and fish, your favourite dish?
In your best suit, is it best to teat fruit?
Should champagne, be drunk on a train?
Is it right, to eat meat at night?
Should I compose a ballad, whilst eating a salad?
Would it be misconstrued, or considered quite rude,
to suggest that food, should be eaten whilst nude?
and would it be lewd and incredibly crude,
to drink also beer, recently brewed?
Wedding banquet, Christmas dinner,
eaten by saints, or unrepentant sinner.
Breakfast, dinner and tea, it's easy to see,
and it must be obvious to both you and me,
that food is quite glorious,
if eaten when victorious,

or just sit down and savour, the delicious flavour,
of a simple meal, that's foods appeal,
because when unwell, I've heard tell,
food can be quite healing,
now isn't that just so appealling?
For regardless of wealth, food maintains health,
so eat, drink and be merry,
enjoy our pie of blackberry,
and your brandy made with cherry.
A bottle of wine, now that would be fine,
washed down with a coffee, followed by toffee.
And so I'll conclude, not wanting to be rude,
by suggesting a glutton, will eat too much mutton,
so don't overeat, your pudding and meat,
or you'll just get fat, like an enormous cat,
you'll end up a hog, or an overweight dog.
I'll finally state, you'll get overweight.
So eat your cake, and when you bake,
curb your appetite, you know it's right.
And when you drink, remember to think,
that in excess, or under duress,
drunk or sober, when your life is over,
there may be a banquet in heaven,
for those who care, or even dare,
to spare a thought, whilst meat a-carving,
for the hungry, poor and starving.

LIVING IN DEVON

When I'm 67
I'm going to live in Devon
When I reach 88
I might often turn up late
Now I'm 53
I'll go on a spending spree
When I was 41
girlfriends, I had none
but when I was 20
females, there were plenty
When I was roughly 30
sometimes I was rude and flirty.
People said I was odd
when at 30 I found God
But when I got to 40
I wasn't very naughty
Perhaps when I was 50
I was a bit mean and thrifty
If I reach 99
I'll certainly wine and dine
I hope when I'm 66
I won't need zimmers and sticks
If I die at 67
I wonder, will I go to heaven?
Perhaps I won't live in Devon.
When I reach 64will there be many years more?
Will I be an old bore
who is destitute and poor?
Will I have wit and humour
will people spread a rumour
I hope I won't have a tumour.
When I'm 98
what will be my fate?

GORBACHEV

I said unto the vicar, "Vicar now that I have you in my confidence I feel I can say unto you in complete sincerity: "Would you like to come home and see my Gorbachev?'"

The vicar seemed perplexed and in his confusion did sayeth in reply, "I beg your pardon, what kind of man do you think I am?"

"Vicar, vicar," I intoned, "Lest there be no confusion, I think thou hast misinterpreted my generous offer, let me reassure you, Gorbachev's are very tame and affable creatures."

The vicar coloured, discomfited by his discomfombobulation and released an unpleasant smell, thus confirming my theory that high church Christians are mainly to blame for global warming.

Gathering his wits, or what remained of them, he rallied and in his fruitiest voice did bellow forth, "My good man I should be delighted to come and see your Gorbachev!"

Ten minutes later, chez moi, I could hear the Gorbachev scrabbling at the door as I inserted the key.

"Fear not vicar," I said, "he may paw you a bit but he's really of no threat."

As the vicar entered the sacred portal of my hallowed abode, he did exclaim, "My word sir, I say, what a lovely Gorbachev!"

"Yes quite a magnificent creature resplendent with authentic birthmark."

"Where on earth did you acquire such a prize specimen, surely they are extremely rare?"

"Oh I have contacts amongst the emigré community, in fact it was the Russian oligarch Avram Abramofilch who established a breeding programme using imported stock."

"By jove," said the vicar, "Do you think you could get me one?"

"Oh good heavens no vicar, they're extremely rare and I'm sure that the outlay would be excessive. Perhaps I could arrange for you to be furnished with a Thatcher?"

"Good God man I could not contemplate such a thing. They're very temperamental creatures and I believe extremely hard to train."

"Yes you believe correctly, they're somewhat akin to a Widdecombe. We used to have a Widdecombe you know, but the neighbours complained, and we had to let her go."

"Perhaps you could suggest another breed?" inquired the vicar.

"Well Afghans are a bloody nuisance as you well know. And if I was to get you a Balls, it would have to be a pair, they fret terribly if left alone."

"Yes," interrupted the vicar, "I used to have a pair of Balls but the wife used to abuse them and one day they just weren't there anymore. She refused to reveal their fate even under torture."

"Well that settles it," I replied, "It will have to be a Mandelson."

"Good God man, do you take me for a fool. Do you want for me to be ostracised by the whole community? The Bishop might get to hear. I could even be excommunicated. A Mandelson is out of the question!"

"I quite see your point vicar, forgive my impetuosity I should have realised that for a man in your position a Mandelson is out of the question. Let me see: Osbournes are a bit of a damn nuisance. What about a Cameron?"

"By jove sir, I think you've hit the nail on the head. Camerons are damn fine animals. Could you possibly acquire one for me?"

"Yes indeed vicar. Indeed at this moment there is said to be a glut of Camerons all very reasonably priced."

The vicar was overjoyed, elated even. Perhaps a shade jealous because access to a Gorbachev had been denied, but a look of satisfaction spread across his visage.

The vicar began to jump up and down in glee, playfully intoning, "I'm getting a Cameron, I'm getting a Cameron."

Jesus did say we should retain the enthusiasm and innocence of children but I think the vicar was going too far in this instance.

"Calm down vicar," I suggested, "Your behaviour could be construed as unseemly and inappropriate to a man of your calling."

"Why don't you just bog off! Can't a man of staid and repressed emotions show a little enthusiasm now and again. Just make sure I get my Cameron soon young man, or I'll unleash the wrath of God upon you!"

"Yes vicar. Of course vicar," I said, patting the Gorbachev on the head. The vicar usually got the upper hand, but he hadn't got a Gorbachev, had he?

FIGHT NIGHT

Gloria Glook was a stunner, but she had very few brains. In fact she only had one, which was a K.46 model, making her a very, very dumb blonde.

Her main aim in life was to date a rich footballer and become a WAG. Her main advantage in this respect is that sexually she was 'easy'; in fact not only easy, but positively a pushover. Unfortunately she had got pregnant to the very stupid Wayne, who had exaggerated his football 'talent', roughly by a factor of 1 million give or take 4 or 5.

Now, Wayne was a 'ladies man'. You might say he was good looking if your eyesight was poor or you were a dumb blonde, but in his own mind he was 'God's gift' to womankind, and Wayne had set his sights on Chardonnay, whose brain was a K.46+0.1 model, making her a dumb brunette. Naturally she fell for Wayne's 'charms' and also ended up pregnant.

Wayne was now well on his way to populating the planet with stupid children, thus ensuring gainful employment to ASBO issuers well up until the time of the 'second coming'. However, as this story is not another excuse for religious speculation, I shall terminate the religious speculation.

Suffice it to say that when Gloria discovered the existence of Chardonnay and Wayne's talent for human reproduction, of an inferior quality, the ensuing 'Big Fight' between Gloria and Chardonnay was screened on Sky pay for view for £50 per household.

Rupert Murdoch never misses a trick with dumb blondes, brunettes and even dumber television punters!

THE JESUS JOKE BOOK!

The Jesus Joke Book was brought to me by an angel, riding a camel from the east. Or was it given to me by a drunkard in a pub, saying, "£100 guvnor for pure prophetic gold." I don't know, I can't remember, but what I do know is that Jesus must have had the occasional chortle.

The Jesus Joke Book: Passed down through mysterious secret societies and kept hidden from the general public for nearly 2 millenia, the Jesus Joke Book will have you rolling in the aisles, tittering in the temples, chortling in the chantry and guffawing in the gloom of a musty monastery. With marvellous jokes such as:

Did you hear the one about the three rabbis?

What's the difference between a Greek, a Jew and a Philistine?

What about the portly pharisee who went on holiday to Portugal?

and many other rip-roaring, rib-tickling classics.

All jokes are strictly kosher, although Muslims might not get all of them.

Write on vellum parchment, get the Jesus Joke Book at all discount discredited booksellers for the bargain price of £24.99.

What better present for Christmas than the jokes of Christ Himself? Yes, the Jesus Joke Book would make an excellent stocking filler. Put the funny side of Christ into your Christmas and have a very merry Christmas. Get the Jesus Joke Book or suffer eternal damnation!

FAT CAT

My cat
is very fat.
It used to chase the mice
which wasn't very nice.
It used to harass the birds
and I used scolding words.
Now it just sits on the window sill
after it's early morning sickness pill
and all day long it snoozes
dreaming up cunning ruses.
Food is it's ultimate goal
as it slinks to the dinner bowl.
Then on the mat it sits
until it goes outside and spits
it can't even be bothered with blue tits.
No wonder it's so obese!
Should I alert the animal police?
My cat, who is very fat,
snoozes comfortably on the mat.

RUPERT AND THE AU PAIR

Rupert bear didn't have a care,
he rarely combed his hair.
Sometimes he'd sit and stare.
He dreamt of an affair,
with Cynthia, née Blair.
Perhaps it's for a dare,
but he was rejected, how unfair!
So he employed an au pair,
who was extraordinarily rare,
because she agreed to an affair.
Now Rupert combs his hair!

THE FRIDGE MONSTER

When I opened the fridge door
I was hoping to see a food store
What I saw left me in shock
there was nothing left to add to the wok.
Instead I saw a great fat thing,
the fridge monster started to sing.

I asked him what he was doing there.
He said, "I really don't care."
"Have you eaten all my food?
Because that would be greedy and rude."
At that moment he opened his big fat mouth,
and out came a liquid jet heading north and south.

Prawns and cream and bacon and eggs,
he surely must have hollow legs,
then out came mushrooms and leftover dregs.
I grabbed him by his big fat snout.
I opened the door and threw him out.
I hope he dies with painful gout!

CAMILLA (THE GORILLA)

When I walked in the house, she was dressed as a gorilla,

I said she was stupid, and that I might kill her.

I said, "Have you been cooking, what's for dinner?"

She said, "If you weren't so fat, you'd be a lot thinner!"

I said, "Is it any wonder our kids are so stupid?"

She said, "When I met you, I was mesmerised by cupid.

She said, "Your mother should have brought you up better."

I said, "I wish I'd just used a french letter."

She said, "Why must we row?'

I said, "Because you're a cow."

Anyway, to cut a long story short,

that's the reason why we ended in court.

And finally we got the divorce,

I have to admit, to a level of remorse.

That on that day, my wife Camilla,

was stupid enough to dress as a gorilla!

THE BLEEDING DOCTOR

I was bleeding from my nose
I was bleeding from my head
I was bleeding from my shoulder
I must be bleeding dead!
I went to see the doctor.
He said, "You're a bleeding fool."
I asked him what he meant.
He said, "You shouldn't have fallen from the mule."
I said, "You've got it wrong,
you know you are of course,
it wasn't a mule that threw me,
the fall was from a horse."
"Nevertheless," the doctor told me,
"You could have avoided the fall,
you're really very sill,
you shouldn't have been riding at all."
"Listen," I told the doctor,
"I appreciate the advice,
just try and make me better,
your comments aren't too nice."

David Wilding, 2009

PROVERBS

A man with a gun looks more primitive than an ape.

A bigot has suspended the search for truth and justice.

Lies and deceit blacken only you.

A person who has pre-judged his own virtue is inclined to arrogance.

Death surrounds arrogance.

Be respectable but never too respectable not to show disrespect to those who show a lack of respect for others.

Repentance means saying, "Sorry," with the whole of your spirit.

War is an angry response, only diplomacy prevails.

JERUSALEM

The "shining city" on the hill

---------- θ ----------

Where art thou Jerusalem?
the shining vision of spiritual men,
a vision of prosperity and peace,
war is over, the fighting must cease.
Jerusalem can be built on compromise,
that is the truth, that I advise.
If you want to continue in hate,
never to change until it's too late,
throw away the lifeline of salvation,
continue the wars of devastation.
Jerusalem will be built, regardless,
in heaven or on Earth,
join the project, and prove your worth.
Because the time has come, human race,
to prove you're not just a mental case.
Make your peace with man and God,
don't spoil the child, but spare the rod.
Arrogance and prejudice will wither and die,
repent of your sin, Jerusalem is nigh!

David Wilding, May 2006